QUIET

 MEETING

CW00591758

MEETING GOD IN QUIET

Ruth Goring

6 studies for individuals or groups

Scripture Union

Scripture Union, 207-209 Queensway, Bletchley, MK2 2EB, England.
e-mail: info@scriptureunion.org.uk
Internet: http://www.scripture.org.uk/

First published in the United States by InterVarsity Press
First published in Great Britain by Scripture Union, 2000

Cover photograph: Roberta Polfus

ISBN 1 85999 399 0

Printed in Great Britain by Ebenezer Baylis & Son, The Trinity Press, Worcester and
London.

Contents

INTRODUCING
Meeting God in Quiet

A cross stands on a promontory overlooking Campus by the Sea, InterVarsity Christian Fellowship's camp on Catalina Island, off California's southern coast. Yesterday I noticed bird droppings on the cross's horizontal beam and scattered on its base. Today as I approached, a large crow flew off from a perch on its top, just above where the soldiers would have placed Pilate's sign, "JESUS OF NAZARETH, THE KING OF THE JEWS."

Somehow it seems appropriate that birds—even crows, obnoxious as they can be—would find refuge at the cross:

> Even the sparrow has found a home,
> > and the swallow a nest for herself,
> > > where she may have her young—
> a place near your altar,
> > O LORD Almighty, my King and my God. (Psalm 84:3)

I am sometimes like a crow—too noisy, too large, too aggressive. I need the refuge of Jesus' cross. I need to be quieted.

This study guide is an invitation away from the noisiness of our culture and our own hearts, and into the shelter of God's peace. As you will discover, it is actually more than a *study* guide, for it gives you opportunities not only to think about what Scripture says but to let it soak into your life as you practise quietness with God and others.

Henri Nouwen says, "A word with power is a word that comes out of silence. A word that bears fruit is a word that emerges from . . . the divine silence in which love rests secure" (*The Way of the Heart*, p. 56). Come rest in that divine silence, by the sea or in your bedroom, alone in a park or in the midst of a group of seeking friends. God's Word will show the way. God's peace and Jesus' cross will be your refuge.

Practising the Disciplines

Each of the studies focuses on a different spiritual discipline that takes us deeper into the topic.

1. *Scripture study:* we begin with an inductive study that reveals what the Bible has to say about the topic.

2. *Confession:* we look at ourselves in the light of Scripture, taking time in the midst of Bible study for silent reflection and repentance.

3. *Community:* we move to interaction with others around a passage or an exercise, asking for guidance and encouragement as we seek God.

4. *Silence:* again we come before Scripture, but this time seeking not to analyze but to hear God's voice and guidance for us.

5. *Obedience:* in the light of Scripture's teaching we make commitments to change.

6. *Prayer:* we take time to seek God, weaving prayer through our encounter with Scripture.

These sessions are designed to be completed in 45 minutes to an hour in a group, or 30 minutes in personal study. However, feel free to follow the leading of the Holy Spirit and spend as long as is needed on each study.

Every session has several components.

Turning Toward God. Discussion or reflection questions and exercises to draw us into the topic at hand.

Receiving God's Word. A Bible study with application and spiritual exercises.

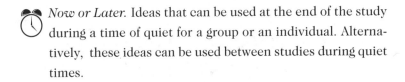 *Now or Later.* Ideas that can be used at the end of the study during a time of quiet for a group or an individual. Alternatively, these ideas can be used between studies during quiet times.

The components of this guide will help you to meet God with both your mind and heart. May you be transformed by his Word as you complete these studies.

1

GOD'S BLESSING OF REST

....

Practising the Discipline of Scripture Study

The Lord "grants sleep to those he loves," the psalmist says (Psalm 127:2). *Sleep.* Not busy religious activity. Not the drugged slumber of those who want only to escape pain. God gives us deep rest that restores our energy and vision.

Thousands of years ago, after the Israelites escaped bondage in Egypt through God's deliverance, they came near to the Promised Land, the land of rest—and said no to God's gift. They didn't trust God to open the way for them. And so, as James Reapsome puts it in *Hebrews* (LBS), "they missed the opportunity for living in God's land of blessing and perished in a wilderness of unbelief and disobedience." The writer of Hebrews considers the Israelites' choice and urges us to choose differently—to follow God into his promised rest.

 TURNING TOWARD GOD ✻What are your hopes as you begin this series of studies and spiritual disciplines focused on quietness?

✽Spend one or two minutes in silence, asking God to begin giving you his rest even as you launch into the study.

The Discipline of Scripture Study

God's Word is one of our greatest resources for knowing him and drawing close to him. What follows is an inductive Bible study that will help you draw out the truths of Scripture for yourself through three types of questions: observation (to gather the facts), interpretation (to discern the meaning) and application (to relate the truths of Scripture to our lives).

 RECEIVING GOD'S WORD   **1.** Read Hebrews 4:1-11. Who is "they" in verse 2? (If needed, skim 3:16-18 for more information.)

How does the writer describe their failure (vv. 2 and 6)?

2. What is the writer's deep concern for his audience (vv. 1 and 11)?

3. God promises us rest in verse 1. How do you respond to that promise?

4. What are the qualities of those who receive God's rest (vv. 2-3)?

5. Summarize the writer's reasoning to back up the claim that God is still offering his people rest, even though the original offer was made to the Israelites thousands of years ago. See verses 3-8.

6. What does it mean to enter *God's* rest?

7. Would we need rest even if the human race had never fallen into sin? Refer to this passage to support your answer.

8. Is failing to rest a sin? Explain your answer.

9. The writer links entering God's rest with having faith (v. 2) and believing (v. 3). Have you experienced this connection in your own life—either positively or negatively? How?

10. What does it mean to rest from our own work "just as God did from his" (v. 10)?

11. What keeps you from entering God's rest?

What steps would you like to take to accept God's invitation to rest?

Offer God praise for the promise of rest and the invitation to experience it more deeply.

NOW OR LATER   Are you living in God's rest? Journal through this question. Consider: Is your sleep usually sound? Do you give your body enough time for the rest it needs? How is your blood pressure? Do you practise regular sabbaths—one day in seven, or the equivalent, given over to worship and rest?

What about your thought life? Do you usually live in God's peace?

If your answers show that you are neglecting rest, ask God that, in the process of completing this study guide, you will be led into greater quietness, peace and awareness of his presence.

2

ACCEPTING OUR LIMITS

....

Practising the Discipline of Confession

In Western nations, highly developed technology surrounds us with the illusion of being able to control our own lives. Because we live in this illusion, we especially hate experiences of helplessness.

Our desire to control our lives sometimes prevents us from experiencing the paradoxical power of the gospel: strength in suffering, in vulnerability.

> The swiftest things are the softest things. A bird is active, because a bird is soft. A stone is helpless, because a stone is hard. The stone must by its own nature go downwards, because hardness is weakness. The bird can of its nature go upwards, because *fragility is force*. . . . Angels can fly because they take themselves lightly. (G. K. Chesterton, *Orthodoxy,* chap. 7, emphasis added)

"Taking ourselves lightly" requires confession of our sins, needs and limitations.

TURNING TOWARD GOD   ✳Recall a time when you felt especially helpless, unable to control the course of your life.

✳Now imagine that you are a film director, planning to depict this moment in your life as a movie scene. What colours would you want for the set and for the actors' clothing? What kind of music would you choose?

The Discipline of Confession

God calls us to confess our sin to him and to one another. Confession is an opportunity to ask for God's help and mercy. Interacting with this Scripture and the voice of the psalmist will help you to open your heart to God. Along the way you will have some opportunities to confess your sin. You may want to do this orally, silently or in writing. Follow God's leading.

 RECEIVING GOD'S WORD   **1.** Read Psalm 86. List the petitions the psalmist makes to God in verses 1-4.

2. How does the psalmist describe himself in these verses?

3. In G. K. Chesterton's terms (see quote on p. 12), would the psalmist here be "hard" or "fragile"? Explain your answer.

4. What characteristics of God are important to the psalmist in this time of need?

5. How do you respond to this picture of God?

6. What particular situation makes David, the psalmist, feel helpless (v. 14)?

7. Is his prayer simply for protection, or does he want God to do something more (v. 11)? Explain.

8. Looking back through the passage, what promises does the psalmist make to God? (Note phrases beginning "I will.")

9. How has his neediness prepared him to experience God's work?

10. Spend some time in quiet. Let God bring to mind all the ways you are in need of mercy: difficult circumstances, human limitations, sin. Speak or write these things to God: "Hear, O LORD, and answer me, for _____."

11. Look back at your answers to question 4. How do these attributes of God meet the needs and lacks you have confessed?

12. Go back to the "movie scene" you imagined in "Turning Toward God." Choose a symbol of hope—the hope of God's forgiveness and faithful response to your need. It might be a flower, a shaft of light or any object that could symbolize God's goodness. Where would you place it in the scene?

Freely express your sense of need for God and your struggles to depend on him.

NOW OR LATER   When we confess our sins to God, it's important to wait for his response. Bring to the Lord any questions you have about the sin you have confessed or other issues that are troubling you. With your journal and pen ready, wait quietly in a posture of listening. Write down any pictures or words that come into your mind.

3

PREPARED TO SERVE

Practising the Discipline of Community

We don't often think of quietness as something that can be practised with others. Usually when we are with another person, we feel that we must be talking or doing something to make our time together significant. But there are other possibilities.

In my community we have returned to the practice of Grand Silence beginning at 9:00 p.m. and continuing until after breakfast the next morning. To be silent alone is one thing, but I have come to love being silent together. To give up words as a community is to attempt to go to the depths together. At breakfast I feel as though we are all waiting together for God's saving touch. There are so many ways we are still unsaved. "It is good to wait in silence for Yahweh to save" (Lam. 3:26). (Macrina Wiederkehr, *A Tree Full of Angels*, pp. 38-39)

The Discipline of Community

God has given us other people in the body of Christ for support and encouragement, as well as enjoyment. As we learn about Christ from Scripture and from each other, we are made complete. For the following exercises and Scripture study you need to work with one or two others or a small group. Ask someone you trust to work through this material with you. (This could include a spouse, but it would be good to include a friend as well.)

TURNING TOWARD GOD ❊What is the balance of noise and quiet in your typical weekday? Make a "sound map" to find out. Shade each hour segment in the two clocks below according to how much noise it usually contains.

white = near silence

light gray = conversation or quiet music

darker gray = layers of noise, such as traffic and car radio, or people conversing in a restaurant that has piped-in music

black = many layers of noise

(You will need to make sure your partners have their own copies of these pages.)

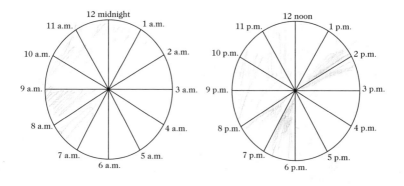

✥Compare your sound map with your companion's. Do your lives seem excessively "dark" (noisy)?

✥Do your white segments represent time that you enjoy or that you dread? Discuss.

 RECEIVING GOD'S WORD   1. Read Mark 6:45-56. What crowd is Jesus dismissing? (If you need a reminder, skim verses 30-44.)

2. Why does Jesus seek quiet and solitude?

3. Imagine yourself in the boat with the disciples, taking turns at the oars. What sounds do you hear in early evening?

How do those sounds change as the night wears on?

What causes you to cry out?

4. Why are the disciples alarmed by Jesus' appearing (vv. 49-52)?

5. How does Jesus' presence meet their shared need?

6. How can Christian groups and communities both long for God's presence and fear it? If possible, give an example from your own experience.

7. What kind of day follows the (mostly) quiet night on the lake?

Describe the scene pictured in verses 54-56.

8. How do times of quiet help us in interacting with others?

9. Look back at "Turning Toward God." How would your sound map be different for Sunday (or whatever day serves as your sabbath)?

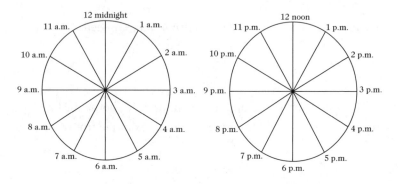

10. Are you regularly experiencing a "quietness-in-community" that (1) allows you to be in God's presence together and (2) replenishes you to face a week of service? Explain.

11. Brainstorm ways that your small group, family or living group could establish or increase times of community silence so as to "go to the depths together."

Pray for each other. Spend at least five minutes in silent listening to God and intercession; then speak the prayers that rise out of your shared quietness.

NOW OR LATER   What friends or family members bring a restful quietness into your life? How is this different from an uncommunicative silence of emotional absence? Journal about someone whose presence, like Jesus', brings peace in your life, or write that person a note of thanks.

4

GIVING UP OUR WORRIES

....

Practising the Discipline
of Silence

Jesus told us not to worry (Matthew 6:25, 34), but most of us have trouble obeying this command. Our minds race with our obligations, our to-do lists, our fears. Our bodies respond with stomach ulcers, insomnia, high blood pressure, and innumerable aches and pains. We need to pay attention to Jesus' words and allow him to minister to our hearts in quietness.

TURNING TOWARD GOD It's likely that as you try to pay attention to the passage below, other thoughts will crowd in. Many of these thoughts come from your worries. So spend five to ten minutes *first* unpacking these worries.

✳Use small sheets of paper, or cut larger sheets into strips. List each worry, large or small, on a separate piece of paper as it comes to mind.

✽ Now sort your worries into two piles: (1) things you can do something about and (2) things that are out of your control. Put the two piles to the side, asking God to watch over these concerns as you read his Word.

The Discipline of Silence

For many of us the disciplines of silence and meditation are the most difficult to pursue. We want to complete a task—read through a book of the Bible or pray through a list of needs. Sometimes, however, God wants us simply to come before him and wait to hear his voice. The Bible study below is best done in quiet, whether you are in a room with others in your small group or alone. After you have completed all of the questions on your own, then you may discuss them with a group.

 RECEIVING GOD'S WORD   1. Read Psalm 9:1-6 through several times.

¹I will praise you, O LORD, with all my heart;
    I will tell of all your wonders.
²I will be glad and rejoice in you;
    I will sing praise to your name, O Most High.

³My enemies turn back;
    they stumble and perish before you.
⁴For you have upheld my right hand and my cause;
    you have sat on your throne, judging righteously.
⁵You have rebuked the nations and destroyed the
    wicked;
    you have blotted out their name for ever and
    ever.

> ⁶Endless ruin has overtaken the enemy,
>   you have uprooted their cities;
>   even the memory of them has perished.

2. Pray for God to guide you to the words or phrases in this passage that you especially need to hear.

3. Read the passage again slowly.

4. What words or phrases stand out to you?

5. Listen silently to God. If you sense that he is speaking, write down what you hear. If not, simply enjoy the silence as a time to be close to him.

6. Go back to your "worry piles"—first, those that are out of your control. How does Psalm 9 speak to you about these "enemies"?

7. You can do something about your other pile of worries, but here too you need God's wisdom. Ask the Holy Spirit for help as you write down one or two simple steps you can take to deal with each of these "enemies" in the near future. Decide which one of these you will work on tomorrow or in the coming week.

Today's Scripture says that God upholds your cause. Thank

him for fighting on your behalf and freeing you from your worries.

NOW OR LATER   Richard Foster *(Meditative Prayer)* suggests putting your worries into an imaginary box as you prepare to pray. It may help even more to have a real box. Try decorating a shoebox or any small box with Scripture verses and symbols. Each day as you spend quiet time with God, write down worries that come to mind and drop them into the box, offering them to the Lord.

Plan to clean out your worry box every month or so, taking out the slips of paper that represent *obsolete* worries—situations where you have seen God "uphold your cause" or those that you have learned to trust him with. Give great thanks as you drop these slips into a paper-recycling bin!

5

MAKING TIME FOR GOD

··

Practising the Discipline of Obedience

Living in greater quietness is not a natural tendency in our noisy culture. But it is essential both in our own discipleship and in our ministry to others, as Henri Nouwen explains in *The Way of the Heart:*

> Our task is to help people concentrate on the real but often hidden event of God's active presence in their lives. Hence, the question that must guide all [ministry] is not how to keep people busy, but how to keep them from being so busy that they can no longer hear the voice of God who speaks in silence. (p. 63)

What is God's call to us? How will we respond?

TURNING TOWARD GOD   ✱Today, begin with silence, just being in God's presence. Welcome him, and be aware of his welcome.

The Discipline of Obedience

God has called us to follow him. Sometimes we deliberately turn away from what we know he wants for us. At other times we wander from him on a gently meandering path. Both are acts of sin that put us out of God's reach. Obedience brings us close to God again. This Bible study and the application questions will help you discover where you need to turn back toward God.

 RECEIVING GOD'S WORD 1. Read Exodus 18. How is God's work emphasized in verses 1-12?

2. How do the names of Moses' sons reflect important elements of God's work?

3. How does Jethro express his newfound understanding of the Lord's supremacy (vv. 10-12)?

4. What problem does Jethro see in Moses' use of time (vv. 13-18)?

5. "The work is too heavy for you; you cannot handle it alone" (v. 18). In what areas of your life do you identify with this statement?

6. What advice does Jethro give Moses (vv. 19-23)?

In New Testament terms, what spiritual gift(s) is Jethro using here?

7. If God offers you an answer to your need, whether through an invitation to trust him more deeply, to share your load with others or simply to give up an activity, are you willing to obey? Spend a little while confronting this question in silence.

8. Spiritual disciplines often interlock with one another. Explain how this story shows Moses practising the disciplines of community and obedience together.

9. Go back to questions 5 and 7 with a prayer partner or your small group, following Moses' example. Pray together, aloud and then in silence, for the areas of life in which you feel overloaded. Then share any wisdom that you sense God is giving you for each other. Keep a humble spirit, like Jethro's ("*if* you do this and God so commands," v. 23).

10. Think about any counsel you have received. If you believe it is indeed from God, what action(s) will you take to obey?

Praise God for the wisdom he gives through the Holy Spirit and through his people. Even if your path is not yet clear, thank him that he will make a way for you to "stand the strain" of life's demands.

NOW OR LATER   As soon as you make a commitment, large or small, to quiet your life as Moses quieted his, make it known to your prayer partner or small group. Be specific! There may be practical ways these friends can begin sharing your load. And they can help you stay faithful to your commitment by asking for periodic reports.

6

BEING RESTORED TO GOD

·····························
Practising the Discipline of Prayer

Quietness is a gift. It allows us to rest and recover balance. It is an essential component of physical and spiritual health. It permits us to go to the depths with God and with each other.

Sometimes quietness is forced on us through circumstances such as illness or an accident. Whether it comes on us or we choose it, it can become an occasion for prayer—as it does for Jonah in today's Scripture text. Even if we experience little immediate reward in such prayer, God always welcomes us into his presence. In the words of St. Julian of Norwich: "For in dryness and in barrenness, in sickness and in feebleness, then is thy prayer well-pleasant to me, though thee thinketh it savour thee nought but little. And so is all thy believing prayer in my sight" (*Revelations of Divine Love*, pp. 44-45).

 TURNING TOWARD GOD ✶Have these studies helped you to welcome times of quietness in the past days and weeks? Explain.

*Spend a minute or two silently "breathing" the Jesus Prayer: "Lord Jesus Christ, have mercy on me, a sinner." Breathing slowly and deeply, let your mind hold the words *Lord Jesus Christ* each time you inhale, then exhale with *Have mercy on me, a sinner.*

The Discipline of Prayer

Prayer draws us close to God. It is an opportunity to give him our concerns and to listen for his voice. In prayer we may not always feel that we have connected with God, but as we remain faithful to seeking him, we will experience the riches of companionship with him. Our desire for and understanding of prayer grow also as we study Scripture.

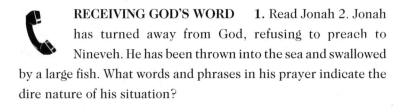 **RECEIVING GOD'S WORD**   **1.** Read Jonah 2. Jonah has turned away from God, refusing to preach to Nineveh. He has been thrown into the sea and swallowed by a large fish. What words and phrases in his prayer indicate the dire nature of his situation?

What words and phrases indicate his gratitude to God?

2. Jonah has been saved from the raging sea, but he's inside a slimy fish—not exactly a comfortable environment. What is surprising about his confidence in God?

3. If you were in Jonah's situation, how might you be speaking to God?

4. When is it hard for you to be quiet in prayer and find rest in God's presence?

5. Jonah has disobeyed God. Why do you think God chooses to return him to dry land (vv. 8-10)?

6. Can you recall a time of enforced quietness when you resorted to prayer because of your great need? How did God rescue you from trouble?

7. Write God a prayer of joy and appreciation for how he has rescued you in the past and for what he is doing in your life now.

Ask God to teach you how to pray. Close your prayer with the words of the psalmist:

Find rest, O my soul, in God alone;
    my hope comes from him.
He alone is my rock and my salvation;
    he is my fortress, I will not be shaken.

My salvation and my honor depend on God;
    he is my mighty rock, my refuge.
Trust in him at all times, O people;
    pour out your hearts to him,
        for God is our refuge. (Psalm 62:5-8)

NOW OR LATER   "It is the aim of contemplative living, at least in the Christian mode, that you learn to recognize a blessing when you see one, and are able to respond to it with words that God has given you" (Kathleen Norris, *The Cloister Walk*, p. 352). Spend half a day, or even a whole day, in a retreat of silence. Bring your Bible, your journal and your "worry box" (see study 4) to a nearby retreat center. Or you could go to a quiet park, a library or a hotel; or ask to use an empty classroom at your church. Meditate on a psalm or two, using the simple format you followed in study 4 (questions 1-5). Focus your prayer on giving thanks to God for his blessings and listening for what he might be saying to you.

Guidelines for Leaders

My grace is sufficient for you. (2 Corinthians 12:9)

If leading a small group is something new for you, don't worry. These sessions are designed to be led easily. As a matter of fact, the flow of questions in the Bible study portions through the passage, from observation to interpretation to application, is so natural that you may feel the studies lead themselves.

You don't need to be an expert on the Bible or a trained teacher to lead a small group discussion. The idea behind these sessions is that the leader guides group members to discover for themselves what the Bible has to say and to listen for God's guidance. This method of learning will allow group members to remember much more of what is said than a lecture would.

This study guide is flexible. You can use it with a variety of groups—student, professional, neighbourhood or church groups. Each study takes forty-five to sixty minutes in a group setting.

There are some important facts to know about group dynamics and encouraging discussion. The suggestions listed below should enable you to fulfill your role as leader effectively and enjoyably.

Preparing for the Study

1. Ask God to help you understand and apply the passage in your own life. Unless this happens, you will not be prepared to lead others. Pray too for the various members of the group. Ask God to open your hearts to the message of his Word and motivate you to action.

2. Read the introduction to the entire guide to get an overview of the issues which will be explored.

3. As you begin each study, read and reread the assigned Bible passage to familiarize yourself with it.

4. This study guide is based on the New International Version of the Bible. It will help you and the group if you use this translation as the basis for your study and discussion.

5. Carefully work through each question in the study. Spend time in meditation and reflection as you consider how to respond.

6. Write your thoughts and responses in the space provided in the study guide. This will help you to express your understanding of the passage clearly.

7. It might help to have a Bible dictionary handy. Use it to look up any unfamiliar words, names or places. (For additional help on how to study a passage, see chapter five of *Leading Bible Discussions*, InterVarsity Press.)

8. Consider how you need to apply the Scripture to your life. Remember that the group will follow your lead in responding to the studies. They will not go any deeper than you do.

Leading the Study

1. Begin the study on time. Open with prayer, asking God to help the group understand and apply the passage.

2. Be sure that everyone in your group has a study guide. There are some questions and activities they will need to work through on their own, either beforehand or during the study session.

3. The flow of each study varies a bit. Many of the studies have time for silent reflection as well as for group discussion. Think through how you will lead the group through the times of silence, and read through the notes for guidance. It can be very powerful to have times of silence in the midst of a group session. Session four in particular focuses on silence and calls for an extended time apart. Then you can come together and share your experiences.

4. At the beginning of your first time together, explain that these studies are meant to be discussions, not lectures. Encourage the members of the group to participate. However, do not put pressure on those who may be hesitant to speak during the first few sessions. You may want to suggest the following guidelines to your group.

☐ Stick to the topic being discussed.

☐ Your responses should be based on the verses that are the focus of the discussion and not on outside authorities such as commentaries or speakers.

☐ These studies focus on a particular passage of Scripture. Only rarely should you refer to other portions of the Bible. This allows for everyone to participate on equal ground and for in-depth study.

☐ Anything said in the group is considered confidential and will not be discussed outside the group unless specific permission is given to do so.

☐ Provide time for each person present to talk if he or she feels comfortable doing so.

☐ Listen attentively to each other and learn from one another.

☐ Pray for each other.

5. Have a group member read the introduction at the beginning of the discussion.

6. Every session begins with the "Turning Toward God" section. The questions or activities are meant to be used before the passage is read. These questions introduce the theme of the study and encourage group members to begin to open up. Encourage as many members as possible to participate, and be ready to get the discussion going with your own response.

7. Either prior to or right after "Turning Toward God," you will see a definition of the specific discipline the session focuses on.

Have someone read that explanation.

8. Have one or more group member(s) read aloud the passage to be studied.

9. As you ask the questions under "Receiving God's Word," keep in mind that they are designed to be used just as they are written. You may simply read them aloud, or you may prefer to express them in your own words.

There may be times when it is appropriate to deviate from the study guide. For example, a question may have already been answered. If so, move on to the next. Alternatively, someone may raise an important question not covered in the guide. Take time to discuss it, but try to keep the group from going off at a tangent.

10. Avoid answering your own questions. If necessary, repeat or rephrase them until they are clearly understood, or point out something you have read in the leader's notes to clarify the context or meaning. An eager group quickly becomes passive and silent if they think the leader will do most of the talking.

11. Don't be afraid of silence in response to the discussion questions. People may need time to think about the question before formulating their answers.

12. Don't be content with just one answer. Ask, "What do the rest of you think?" or "Anything else?" until several people have given answers to the question.

13. Acknowledge all contributions. Try to be affirming whenever possible. Never reject an answer. If it is clearly off-base, ask, "Which verse led you to that conclusion?" or again, "What do the rest of you think?"

14. Don't expect every answer to be addressed to you, even though this will probably happen at first. As group members become more at ease, they will begin to truly interact with each other. This is one sign of healthy discussion.

15. Don't be afraid of controversy. It can be very stimulating.

If you don't resolve an issue completely, don't be frustrated. Move on and keep it in mind for later. A subsequent study may solve the problem.

16. Periodically summarize what the group has said about the passage. This helps to draw together the various ideas mentioned and gives continuity to the study. But don't preach.

17. At the end of the Bible discussion you may want to allow group members a time of quiet to work on an idea under "Now or Later." Then discuss what you experienced. Alternatively, you may want to encourage group members to work on these ideas between meetings. Give an opportunity during the session to allow people to talk about what they are learning.

18. Conclude your time together with conversational prayer, adapting the prayer suggestion at the end of the study to your group. Ask for God's help in following through on the commitments you have made.

19. End on time.

Many more suggestions and helps are found in *Small Group Leader's Handbook* and *The Big Book on Small Groups* (both from InterVarsity Press), or *The Small-Group Leader* and *Small Group Starter Kit* (both from Scripture Union). Reading through one of these books would be worth your time.

Study Notes

Study 1. God's Blessing of Rest. Hebrews 4:1-11.
Purpose: To discover God's biblical promise of rest for us.
Question 1. Here you might want to open a brief discussion on how lack of faith (v. 2) and lack of obedience (v. 6) are related.
Question 2. Theologian Barnabas Lindars suggests that the "point at issue is a felt need on the part of the readers to resort to Jewish

customs in order to come to terms with their sense of sin against God and need for atonement. . . . [The writer of] Hebrews regards this return to Judaism as virtual apostasy" (*The Theology of the Letter to the Hebrews,* New Testament Theology, Cambridge University Press, 1991, pp. 10-11).

Question 3. Is God's promise of rest only future (in heaven), or is his rest available now? William L. Lane's opinion is that "faith brings into *the present* the reality of that which is future, unseen, or heavenly. For that reason, those who have believed can be said to enter God's rest already" (*Hebrews 1-8,* Word Biblical Commentary 47A, Word, 1991, p. 99, emphasis added).

Question 5. Many years after the Jewish people were settled in the Promised Land, David wrote about God's promised rest as a *future* event (Psalm 95:11). So, the writer of Hebrews reasons, it is an offer that is still open and that applies to all of us. (Raymond Brown, *The Message of Hebrews: Christ Above All,* InterVarsity Press, 1984, p. 89.)

Question 6. The writer is consciously choosing to quote Scripture texts used in Jewish synagogue worship: "Anyone attending a Sabbath evening service in the synagogue would have heard the call to worship from Psalm 95:7b-11, followed immediately by the celebration of God's sabbath rest in Genesis 2:1-3. . . . [So] prompted by the Holy Spirit, the preacher [of Hebrews] invites his friends to conceive of the promised rest of God in terms of the joy with which the gift of the Sabbath is welcomed. . . . It is the prospect of sharing in the inexpressible joy of that ultimate celebration of the mighty works of God, embracing both creation and redemption" (William L. Lane, *Hebrews: A Call to Commitment,* 1985 reprint, Hendrickson, 1994, p. 68).

Question 8. Consider the fact that verses 6 and 11 speak of "disobedience," and that the command to observe sabbath is among the Ten Commandments. You may want to discuss: How can we take this commandment seriously without being legalistic?

Study 2. Accepting Our Limits. Psalm 86.
Purpose: To quiet our hearts as we learn to trust God's goodness.
Turning Toward God. If you are doing this study in a group, you may want to divide into twos or threes and describe your "movie scenes" to one another.
Question 2. Commentator G. A. F. Knight (*Psalms*, Westminster Press, 1983, 2:69) names this "Anybody's Psalm" and quotes a line from a hymn by Annie S. Hawks, "I need thee every hour." The psalm writer does call himself "devoted to you" (v. 2; elsewhere translated "holy" or "godly"), but his other self-references reflect his neediness and insufficiency.
Question 4. See verses 5, 8-9, 13, 15. The writer draws widely from other Scripture to describe God. In fact, "almost every line of this psalm has been lifted out of other psalms . . . or is a quotation from the *Torah*" (the first five books of the Old Testament; Knight, *Psalms,* p. 69). Note especially his use of Exodus 34:6-7 in verses 5 and 15—a description of God's nature that is often echoed throughout Scripture and was probably used as a sort of creed in worship.
Question 6. Knight believes that the enemies cited here are one's "lower nature"—"tendencies," "habits" and "instincts" within ourselves that would devour our soul. He says, "There is no mention of *men* in the Hebrew" (*Psalms,* pp. 70-71). Whether the enemies are outer or inner, the psalmist faces a time of crisis, and his psalm, like others, "[offers] speech when life has gone beyond our frail efforts to control" (Walter Brueggemann, *Praying the Psalms*, Saint Mary's/Christian Brothers, 1986, p. 19).
Question 7. "The life of faith does not protect us from the pit. Rather, the power of God brings us out of the pit to new life which is not the same as pre-pit existence" (Brueggemann, *Psalms,* p. 44).

It may help to ask, How does the psalmist show that he wants to be *changed* by God?

Question 9. Brueggemann emphasizes that the psalms are our opportunity to bring our "raw hurts, . . . primitive passions, and . . . naive elations . . . into the open, frightening, healing world of speech with the Holy One" (*Praying the Psalms,* p. 20).

Question 10. If you are leading a group, give a good amount of time for silence here, five to ten minutes. If you have the space available, members may even want to move to other rooms to have solitude.

Study 3. Prepared to Serve. Mark 6:45-56.

Purpose: To introduce the practice of quiet in a community setting.

Turning Toward God. If you are leading a group, you may want to ask members to come with their circles completed and then spend five minutes interacting with one another in pairs. Alternatively, you may want to complete the exercise at the beginning of the meeting. It will take about fifteen minutes.

Question 1. After the feeding of the five thousand, "Jesus recognized the rising tide of emotion in the crowd. They were looking for a warrior-Messiah. Perhaps Jesus could sense Satan's temptation that he had faced once before in the wilderness: the prospect of power on earth here and now (Mark 1:13)" (Philip Comfort, ed., *Life Application Bible Commentary,* Tyndale House, 1994, p. 185). So Jesus dismisses the crowd quickly.

Question 3. "Fourth watch of the night" is the period between 3:00 and 6:00 a.m. Though the text does not say, it is likely that the disciples spent most of the night in silence, since they were tired and needed to focus their strength on rowing. Certainly no conversation is recorded.

Notice what terrifies them: it is not their struggle against the "strong wind" but Jesus' appearance on the water.

Question 4. "The Greek word for 'ghost' used here is *phantasma,* meaning an apparition or spectre. The word was associated with magic and charms," as opposed to *pneuma,* which could refer to the "disembodied spirit of someone who had died" (Comfort, ed., *Life Application Bible Commentary,* p. 188).

Did Jesus mean to walk past the beleaguered disciples, ignoring their plight? "It is very likely that . . . 'he intended to pass by them' [means] that he intended to make himself visible to the disciples to relieve their fear and to reveal his power to them" (Larry W. Hurtado, *Mark,* Good News Commentary, Harper & Row, 1983, p. 91).

Question 5. "The ship came to represent for Christians the community of the disciples; they are gathered with Jesus in the ship, the church. The deliverance on the lake then represents the deliverance which Jesus brings to believers in the storms or persecutions which affect the ship of the church" (Ernest Best, *Mark: The Gospel as Story,* Studies of the New Testament and Its World, T & T Clark, 1983, p. 61).

Question 7. Note that the disciples end up at Gennesaret instead of their intended destination, Bethsaida. Probably the winds had blown them off course.

The touching of the edge (sometimes translated "fringe") of Jesus' cloak likely had special meaning: "Jewish men wore tassels on the hem of their robes, according to God's command (Deuteronomy 22:12). By Jesus' day, these tassels were seen as signs of holiness (Matthew 23:5). It was natural that people seeking healing should reach out and touch these" (Comfort, ed., *Life Application Bible Commentary,* p. 192).

Question 9. Watch your time; this question will require a bit of extra time as people fill in their clocks.

Study 4. Giving Up Our Worries. Psalm 9:1-6.

Purpose: To practise meditative listening to Scripture as we release our worries to God.

General Note. If you are leading a group, consider meeting in a setting that will allow you to separate for quiet reflection—for example, at a church or in a quiet park. Open with prayer and perhaps some worshipful singing. Then give people forty-five minutes to an hour to work through the material in "Turning Toward God" and "Receiving from God." Come together afterward to talk about what you experienced and how God spoke through the passage.

Questions 2-4. The following thoughts from various writers may help your meditation.

C. S. Lewis speaks of the joy exemplified in Psalm 9:1-2 as an "appetite for God" that should inform our worship: "an experience fully God-centred, asking of God no gift more urgently than His presence, the gift of Himself, joyous to the highest degree, and unmistakably real" (*Reflections on the Psalms*, Harcourt Brace, 1958, pp. 51-52).

"The two chief springs of praise [in verses 1-2 are] God's actions and His person. . . . *Wonderful deeds* (or things) is a single Hebrew word, particularly frequent in the Psalms, used especially of the great redemptive miracles (*e.g.* 106:7, 22), but also of their less obvious counterparts in daily experience (*cf.* 71:17), and of the hidden glories of Scripture (119:18)" (Derek Kidner, *Psalms 1-72: An Introduction and Commentary on Books I and II of the Psalms*, Inter-Varsity Press, 1973, p. 69).

David's "thought leaps ahead from his own story (*my enemies, my just cause,* 3f.) to what it prefigures: God's total victory . . . and reign of justice, world-wide and everlasting" (Kidner, *Psalms 1-72*, p. 69).

"The true believer hates powerfully and finds a community with Yahweh (the God of Israel) who also hates" (Brueggemann,

Praying the Psalms, p. 60). We tend to be uncomfortable with the
psalmists' talk of hatred, enemies and vengeance. But do we really
want a God who does not hate evil? Such a God would never rise
up against oppression, enslavement, violence, the abuse of
children. We would be left without hope of ultimate justice. So "to
affirm that vengeance belongs to God is an act of profound faith"
(ibid., p. 72).

Study 5. Making Time for God. Exodus 18.
Purpose: To move toward life changes—opening space for quiet in
our lives—in response to Scripture and God's guidance.
Question 1. Notice the repeated phrase "everything God had
done" (vv. 1 and 8) and the emphasis on how Israel was rescued
from Egypt (vv. 1, 8, 9-10).
Question 2. This question can readily be answered from the text,
but following is some information for group members who may be
curious about Moses' family. Exodus 2:15-22 and 4:18-26 tell us
more about Moses' wife, sons and in-laws. Note that since Moses
escaped from Pharaoh *twice* (once after he killed an Egyptian and
again, many years later, when God used him to deliver the Hebrew
people), Eliezer's name does not necessarily imply that he was
born after the crossing of the Red Sea.

There may be a question about the name of Moses' father-
in-law:

> In [Genesis 2] Moses' father-in-law was called Reuel, while here he
> is referred to as Jethro and in Numbers 10:29 as Hobab (see Judg
> 4:11). The difficulty can be resolved once the ambiguity of the ter-
> minology is recognized. The term designating male in-laws is non-
> specific. The term referred to a woman's male relatives and could be
> used for her father, brother or even grandfather. Most solutions take
> account of this. Perhaps Reuel is the grandfather head of the clan,
> Jethro is the father of Zipporah and technically the father-in-law of

Moses, and Hobab is the brother-in-law of Moses, Jethro's son. Alternatively, Jethro and Hobab could both be brothers-in-law, and Reuel the father. (John H. Walton and Victor H. Matthews, *The IVP Bible Background Commentary: Genesis—Deuter-onomy*, Inter-Varsity Press, 1997, p. 87)

Moses was descended from Jacob's son Levi, and we learn from 1 Chronicles 23:14-17 that Moses' sons were counted as part of the tribe of Levi, designated to minister to God. Apparently then, though Exodus 18 doesn't say, Gershom and Eliezer remained with the Israelites rather than returning to Midian with Jethro.

Question 3. Jethro, priest of a Canaanite religion, here joins a significant line of Old Testament Gentiles (for example, Melchizedek, Hagar, Eliezer the servant of Abraham, Rahab, Ruth) who acknowledge and even come into relationship with the God of Abraham, Isaac and Jacob.

The Septuagint (Greek translation of the Old Testament) translates "was delighted" in verse 9 as "was astonished," which well expresses the wonder Jethro must have felt on hearing of God's great deliverance of Israel.

Question 4. "Justice was regarded as a gift from God so that the right decision in settling a legal dispute was to be obtained from him. . . . [Moses'] experience and possession of the spirit of God enabled him to pronounce a right verdict" (Ronald Clements, *Exodus,* Cambridge Bible Commentary, Cambridge University Press, 1972, p. 109). Clearly the weight of this responsibility for the thousands of Israelite migrants is too crushing for Moses to bear alone.

Question 6. Compare Numbers 11:16-17, 24-30, where Moses similarly picks elders to help him; they then receive a portion of his spirit and begin to prophesy. This theme of choosing apprentices to carry on God-given work is also seen in Elijah's choosing of

Elisha and Jesus' choosing of the Twelve.

New Testament lists of spiritual gifts can be found in Romans 12:6-8, 1 Corinthians 12:28 and Ephesians 4:11.

Question 7. If you are leading a group, ask them to reflect on this in silence for a few minutes before discussing this question.

Question 8. The church father Origen notes Moses' humility here: "When I perceive that Moses the prophet full of God, to whom God spoke 'face to face,' accepted counsel from Jethro the priest of [Midian], my mind goes numb with admiration. . . . He did not say, . . . 'How shall I receive counsel from a man, and a Gentile at that, an alien from the people of God?' But he listens and does everything which he says" (*Homilies on Genesis and Exodus,* trans. Ronald E. Heine, Fathers of the Church 71, Catholic University of America Press, 1981, pp. 363-64). Apparently Moses believes that God has spoken through Jethro, and thus he readily obeys.

Question 9. Allow ten to twelve minutes for people to talk and pray through this.

Study 6. Being Restored to God. Jonah 2.
Purpose: To recognize and give thanks for God's ongoing work of grace in our lives.

Question 1. Jacques Ellul points out that in this psalm "everything relating to the abyss is in the past tense," reminding us that sin and the devil have already done their worst, while "the divine action described in the story is at one and the same time both past and future. . . . [God's work] is a majestic adventure which moves on to its consummation by ways which are constantly renewed by God's love" (*The Judgment of Jonah,* trans. Geoffrey W. Bromiley, Eerdmans, 1971, pp. 52-54).

Question 2. Some critics say that because this song speaks of God's deliverance as already received, it could not have been sung by Jonah while still in the fish. But Ellul thinks it reflects Jonah's rediscovery of God's character before deliverance is complete: "Jonah, even while he is not saved, even while he is at the nadir of his misery, in hell, suddenly rediscovers the permanence of grace. . . . In his return to God he comes to know God again" (*Judgment of Jonah,* pp. 48-49).

Another way to look at it: despite Jonah's discomfort, he is aware that the fish is God's means of deliverance from drowning, and this gives him confidence to expect full deliverance back to land (see Terence Fretheim, *The Message of Jonah: A Theological Commentary,* Augsburg, 1997, pp. 96-97).

Question 4. Your struggles here may relate to circumstances (crises or long-term stress), personality (perhaps you tend to be hard-driving and tense) or state of obedience (when you persist in turning away from God, it's hard to relax in his presence).

Question 5. "God has delivered Jonah quite apart from the question of justice. If one were to ask into Jonah's . . . *just* reward, given his disobedience, then God should *not* have had pity. But God's saving action moves beyond the question of justice" (Fretheim, *Message of Jonah,* p. 93). Remember too that in rescuing Jonah, God is following through on his intention to show mercy to Nineveh.

Question 7. If you are leading a group, you may want to ask each person to read aloud his or her prayer when you are done.

Prayer. Allow plenty of time to pray at the end of the study as well.

For Further Reading
G. K. Chesterton, *Orthodoxy,* Twentieth Century Christian Classics, Hodder & Stoughton, 1996.

Richard Foster, *Meditative Prayer,* InterVarsity Press, 1983.

Julian of Norwich, *Revelations of Divine Love,* Hodder & Stoughton, 1987.

Kathleen Norris, *The Cloister Walk,* Riverhead (USA), 1996.

Henri Nouwen, *The Way of the Heart: Desert Spirituality and Contemporary Ministry*, Daybreak, 1990.

Macrina Wiederkehr, *A Tree Full of Angels: Seeing the Holy in the Ordinary*, HarperSanFrancisco (USA), 1988.